Holidays

Halloween

by Rebecca Pettiford

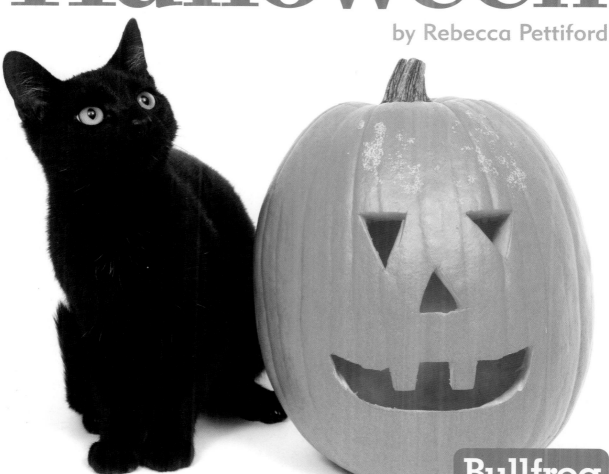

Bullfrog
Books

Ideas for Parents and Teachers

Bullfrog Books let children practice reading informational text at the earliest reading levels. Repetition, familiar words, and photo labels support early readers.

Before Reading
• Discuss the cover photo. What does it tell them?

• Look at the picture glossary together. Read and discuss the words.

Read the Book
• "Walk" through the book and look at the photos. Let the child ask questions. Point out the photo labels.

• Read the book to the child, or have him or her read independently.

After Reading
• Prompt the child to think more. Ask: Does your family celebrate Halloween? What sorts of things do you see when it's Halloween?

Bullfrog Books are published by Jump!
5357 Penn Avenue South
Minneapolis, MN 55419
www.jumplibrary.com

Library of Congress Cataloging-in-Publication Data

Pettiford, Rebecca.
Halloween / by Rebecca Pettiford.
    pages cm. — (Holidays)
"Bullfrog Books."
Includes index.
ISBN 978-1-62031-185-1 (hardcover: alk. paper) —
ISBN 978-1-62496-272-1 (ebook)
1. Halloween—Juvenile literature. I. Title.
GT4965.P428 2015
394.2646—dc23

2014041411

Editor: Jenny Fretland VanVoorst
Series Designer: Ellen Huber
Book Designer: Michelle Sonnek
Photo Researcher: Michelle Sonnek

Photo Credits: All photos by Shutterstock except: age fotostock, 5, 8–9; Corbis, 4, 6–7, 13, 18–19, 20–21, 23tl; iStock, 3; Thinkstock, 17, 22, 23br.

Printed in the United States of America at Corporate Graphics in North Mankato, Minnesota.

Table of Contents

What Is Halloween?

Halloween is October 31.

It is a fun holiday.

Many people celebrate it.

How do we have fun?

We decorate our yard.

What do you see?

Orange pumpkins.
Black cats. Spiders.

Lucy carves a pumpkin.
Papa helps.
They dig out the seeds.
They cut a face.

seeds

Candles light
our pumpkins.

They glow. Spooky!

Mom makes candy apples. Yum!

We frost treats.

Don't touch!

They are for the party.

The party starts.
We eat cookies.
We bob for apples.

cookies

We wear costumes.

Mavis is a witch.

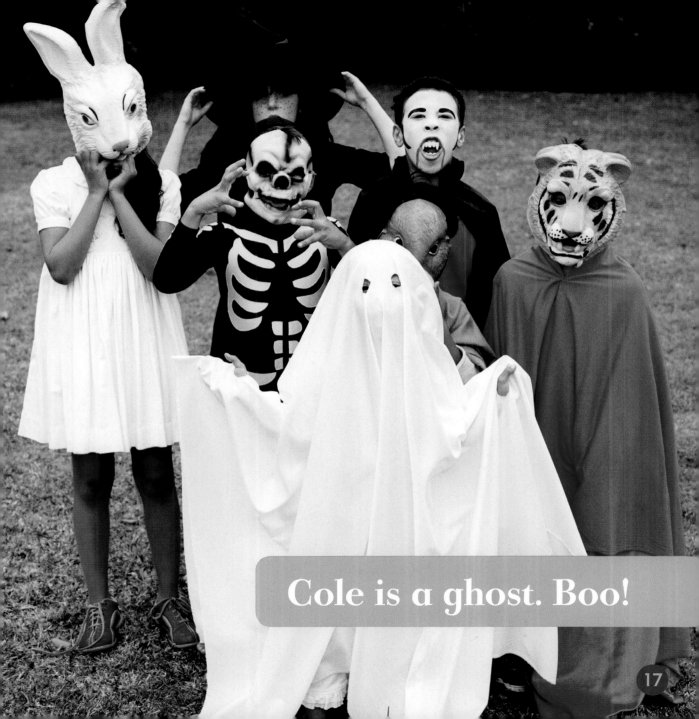

Cole is a ghost. Boo!

Time to go!
We walk to a house.

We ring the bell.
Mrs. Bram answers.

We cry "Trick or treat!"
We get candy.

Halloween is fun!

Symbols of Halloween

black cats

Halloween candy

glowing pumpkins

spooky ghosts

Picture Glossary

bob
To move your
head up and
down in order
to grab an apple
with your teeth.

candy apples
Apples covered
in a sticky
caramel or a
hard cooked
sugar coating.

carve
To cut
something.

costumes
Clothes that
make you look
like something
or someone else.

Index

To Learn More

Learning more is as easy as 1, 2, 3.

1) Go to www.factsurfer.com

2) Enter "Halloween" into the search box.

3) Click the "Surf" button to see a list of websites.

With factsurfer.com, finding more information is just a click away.

DATE DUE

OCT 0 5			
OCT 2 0			
			PRINTED IN U.S.A.